KS2 MATHS

Ages 7-9

Paul Broadbent

PaRragon

Bath · New York · Singapore · Hong Kong · Cologne · Delhi · Melbourne

Educational consultant: Ann Dicks
Illustrated by Rob Davis/www.the-art-agency.co.uk
and Tom Connell/www.the-art-agency.co.uk

This edition published by Parragon in 2010

Parragon
Queen Street House
4 Queen Street
Bath BA1 1HE, UK

ISBN 978-1-4075-3783-2

Printed in China

Notes to parents

The Gold Stars® Key Stage 2 series

The Gold Stars® Key Stage 2 series has been created to help your child revise and practise key skills and information learned in school. Each book is a complete companion to the Key Stage 2 curriculum and has been written by an expert team of teachers. The books will help to prepare your child for the SATS tests that they take in Year 6.

The books also support Scottish National Guidelines 5-14.

How to use this book

• Do talk about what's on the page. Let your child know that you are sharing the activities. Talking about the sections that introduce and revise essential information is particularly important. Usually children will be able to do the fill-in activities fairly independently.

• Keep work times short. Do leave a page that seems too difficult and return to it later.

• It does not matter if your child does some of the pages out of turn.

• Your child may need some extra scrap paper for working out on some of the pages.

• Check your child's answers using the answer section on pages 60-63. Give lots of praise and encouragement and remember to reward effort as well as achievement.

• Do not become anxious if your child finds any of the pages too difficult. Children learn at different rates.

Contents

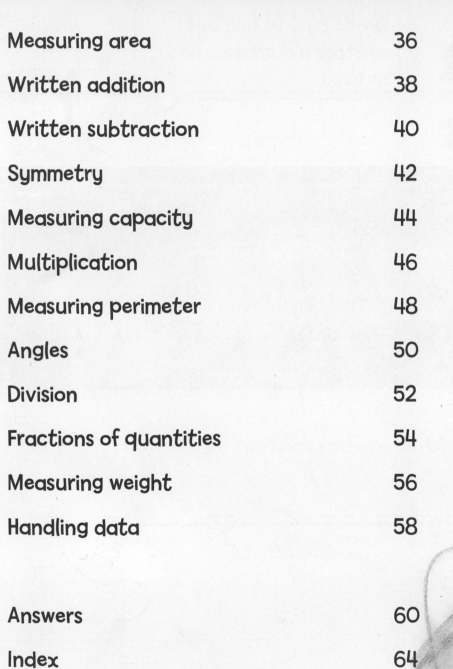

Odd and even numbers

Learning objective: To recognize odd and even numbers.

Odd numbers always end in:

| 1 | 3 | 5 | 7 | 9 |

Even numbers always end in:

| 0 | 2 | 4 | 6 | 8 |

Divide by 2 to find out whether a number is odd or even.

13	21	16	20
* * * * * * * * * * * * * *	* * * * * * * * * * * * * * * * * * * *	* * * * * * * * * * * * * * * *	* * * * * * * * * * * * * * * * * *

Odd numbers always have 1 left over.
Even numbers can be put into 2 equal groups.

A

Join each of these numbers with a line to the correct box.

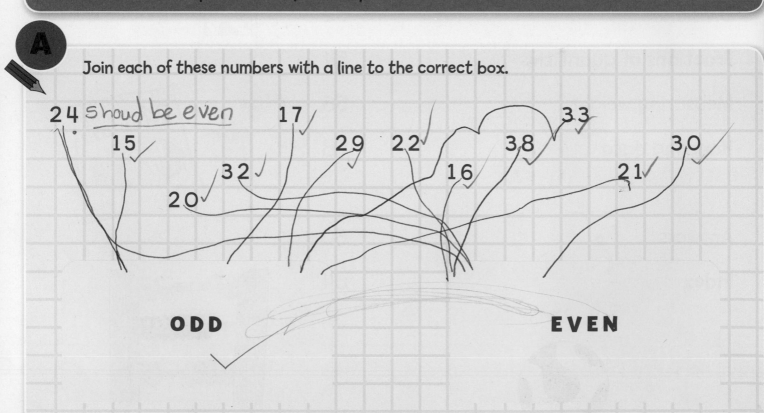

24 shoud be even   17   33
15   29   22   38   30
32   16   21
20

ODD   EVEN

DEFINITION

odd number A number that when divided by 2 has a remainder of 1.

B

Circle all the odd numbers and underline all the even numbers.

(1) 2 (3) 4 (5) 6 (7) 8 (9) 10 (11) 12 (13) 14 (15) 16 (17) 18 (19) 20

1. What is the next odd number after 10?   _11_ ✓

2. What is the next even number after 10?   _12_ ✓

3. What is the next odd number after 15?   _17_ ✓

4. What is the next even number after 14?   _16_ ✓

5. What is the next odd number after 20?   _21_ ✓

No matter how big they are, every single number except 0 is either odd or even. Is 234,456,789 odd or even?

C

Write the next two numbers in these sequences.

1. 28 30 32 34 _36_ _38_ ✓

2. 19 21 23 25 _27_ _29_ ✓

3. 44 46 48 50 _52_ _54_ ✓

4. 25 27 29 31 _33_ _35_ ✓

Pluce Value

Learning objective: To learn how 3-digit numbers are made.

3-digit numbers are made from hundreds, tens and ones.

Look at this number and how it is made:

593

five hundred and ninety-three

593 =
500 + 90 + 3

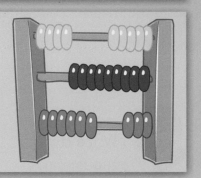

The position of a digit in a number is really important. 359 and 593 use the same digits but are different numbers. The position of the digits 0 to 9 gives the value of the number.

A

Write how many hundreds, tens and ones there are in each of these 3-digit numbers.

1. 398 = _300_ + _90_ + _8_ ✓

2. 217 = _200_ + _10_ + _7_ ✓

3. 452 = _400_ + _50_ + _2_ ✓

4. 683 = _600_ + _80_ + _3_ ✓

5. 165 = _100_ + _60_ + _5_ ✓

6. 709 = _700_ + _00_ + _9_ ✓

B

Write the missing numbers or words to complete each of these.

1. 9 4 1 → nine hundred and ___fourty one___ ✓

2. ___326___ ✓ → three hundred and twenty-six

3. 5 3 4 → ___five hundred and thirty four___ ✓

4. 8 7 0 → ___eight hundred and seventy___ ✓

5. ___219___ ✓ → two hundred and nineteen

6. ___650___ ✓ → six hundred and fifty

C

Write the numbers shown on each abacus. The first one is done for you.

1. 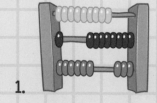 ___83___ ✓

2. 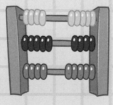 ___545___ ✓

3. 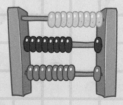 ___911___ ✓

4. 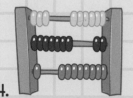 ___628___ ✓

5. 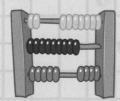 ___704___ ✓

6. 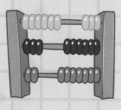 ___367___ ✓

Ordering numbers

Learning objective: To compare 3-digit numbers and put them in order.

> is the sign for 'is more than'.

< is the sign for 'is less than'.

= is the sign for 'is equal to'.

198 > 168

198 is more than 168.

126 < 211

126 is less than 211.

You can remember which sign is which by looking at the shape. When we write 198 > 168, then the sign is wider next to the larger number and narrower next to the smaller number.

You have to compare each digit in numbers to order them.

A Complete each sentence writing the two numbers in the correct place.

1.	147	152	147 is less than 152 .
2.	479	476	476 is less than 479 .
3.	735	753	753 is more than 735 .
4.	381	521	521 is more than 381 .
5.	390	190	190 is less than 390 .
6.	214	244	214 is less than 244 .
7.	586	585	586 is more than 585 .
8.	497	592	592 is more than 497 .

ordering numbers Placing numbers in order from the greatest to the smallest, or vice versa.

B

Write in the missing < or > signs for each pair of numbers.

1. 264 __>__ 254

2. 328 __<__ 431

3. 190 __>__ 119

4. 536 __>__ 523

5. 708 __<__ 807

6. 655 __>__ 635

C

Write each group of numbers in order starting with the smallest.

1. 159 191 112 125   __112__ __125__ __159__ __191__

2. 373 387 278 483   __278__ __373__ __387__ __483__

3. 645 668 622 739   __622__ __645__ __668__ __739__

4. 461 416 460 410   __410__ __416__ __460__ __461__

5. 743 778 760 704   __704__ __743__ __760__ __778__

6. 815 309 459 195   __195__ __309__ __459__ __815__

11

Learning objective: To continue number sequences by counting on or back in steps

A number sequence is a list of numbers in a pattern. To find the rule or pattern in a sequence try finding the difference between each number.

$$45 \xrightarrow{+11} 56 \xrightarrow{+11} 67 \xrightarrow{+11} 78 \xrightarrow{+11} 89$$

The rule or pattern is +11.

$$990 \xrightarrow{-10} 980 \xrightarrow{-10} 970 \xrightarrow{-10} 960 \xrightarrow{-10} 950$$

The rule or pattern is -10.

Follow the rule to continue the sequence.

A Write the next two numbers in each sequence.

1. 22   27   32   37   _42_   _47_
2. 85   87   89   91   _93_   _95_
3. 55   52   49   46   _43_   _40_
4. 44   48   52   56   _60_   _64_
5. 100 96   92   88   _84_   _80_
6. 519 509 499 489 _479_ _469_
7. 268 368 468 568 _668_ _768_
8. 931 831 731 631 _531_ _431_

If you find these activities easy peasy, stretch your brain with the next tricky challenges!

B

Write the missing numbers and the rule for each pattern.

1.	70	_85_	100	115	130	_145_	The rule is : _add 15_
2.	650	600	550	_500_	_450_	400	The rule is : _Take away 50_
3.	_943_	843	_743_	643	543	443	The rule is : _Take away 100_
4.	719	_619_	519	_419_	319	219	The rule is : _Take away 100_
5.	_820_	825	830	835	_840_	845	The rule is : _add 5_
6.	462	_472_	482	492	_502_	512	The rule is : _add 10_
7.	133	123	_113_	_103_	93	83	The rule is : _Take away 10_
8.	_512_	515	518	521	524	_527_	The rule is : _add 3_

C

Two numbers in each sequence have been swapped over. Write each correct sequence.

1. | 975 | 985 | 995 | 965 | 955 | 945 | 935 |
| _995_ | _985_ | _975_ | _965_ | _955_ | _945_ | _935_ |

2. | 80 | 180 | 280 | 380 | 680 | 580 | 480 |
| _80_ | _180_ | _280_ | _380_ | _480_ | _580_ | _480_ |

3. | 853 | 855 | 857 | 851 | 849 | 847 | 845 |
| _857_ | _855_ | _853_ | _851_ | _849_ | _847_ | _845_ |

13

3-D solids

Learning objective: To name and describe 3-D solids.

There are 3-D solids all around you.

Prism	Cuboid	Cube	Cone	Sphere

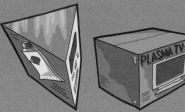

Look at the **faces** of each solid.
This cube has 6 square faces.

Cylinder

Do you know any other examples of 3-D solids?

A Write the name for each shape.

1.  cone

2.  Sphere

3.  Cube

4.  cuboid

5. 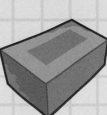 Cylinder

6.  prism

14

DEFINITION

face The flat surface of a solid shape is called a face.

B

Name the shapes in each set and find the odd one out.

1. These shapes are all ___cylinder___.
   The odd one out is a ___cone___.

2. These shapes are all ___Cube___.
   The odd one out is a ___Sphere___.

3. These shapes are all ___Cuboid___.
   The odd one out is a ___prism___.

C

Complete this chart.

Name of shape	cube	cuboid	prism
Total number of faces	6	6	5
Number of square and rectangle faces			
Number of triangular faces			

D

Are these statements **always**, **sometimes** or **never** true?

1. A cuboid has a triangular face. _____

2. A cone has a circle face. _____

3. A cylinder has two circle faces of different sizes. _____

4. A prism has a square face. _____

15

Number trios

Learning objective: To know addition and subtraction facts.

If you know an addition fact, you can work out a related subtraction fact.

Learning number trios is really useful.

Use trios of numbers, such as 11, 4 and 7 to learn the facts.

(11) (4) (7)

$4 + 7 = 11$ $11 - 4 = 7$

$7 + 4 = 11$ $11 - 7 = 4$

Use addition and subtraction facts to help with larger numbers.

$6 + 3 = 9$ $9 - 3 = 6$
$60 + 30 = 90$ $90 - 30 = 60$
$600 + 300 = 900$ $900 - 300 = 600$

A

Write the addition and subtraction families for each trio.

1. 7   8   15

$7 + 8 = 15$ $15 - 7 = 8$
$8 + 7 = 15$ $15 - 8 = 7$

2. 6   12   6

$6 + 6 = 12$ $12 - 6 = 6$
$6 + 6 = 12$ $12 - 6 = 6$

3. 9   14   5

$9 + 5 = 14$ $14 - 5 = 9$
$5 + 9 = 14$ $14 - 9 = 5$

4. 9   7   16

$9 + 7 = 16$ $16 - 9 = 7$
$7 + 9 = 16$ $16 - 7 = 9$

B

Answer these.

1. 6 + 9 = _15_
   60 + 90 = _150_
   600 + 900 = _1,500_

3. 7 + 5 = _12_
   70 + 50 = _120_
   700 + 500 = _1,200_

2. 8 - 4 = _____
   80 - 40 = _____
   800 - 400 = _____

4. 9 - 7 = _____
   90 - 70 = _____
   900 - 700 = _____

C

Write the missing numbers.

1. 6 + [9] = 15

2. 13 - [8] = 5

3. [0] - 9 = 9

4. [4] + 8 = 12

5. 40 + [60] = 100

6. [900] - 200 = 700

7. 80 - [50] = 30

8. [200] + 400 = 600

D

Work these out in your head.

1. What is the sum of 50 and 40?

_____

2. What is the total of 6 and 8?

_____

3. What is the difference between 14 and 7?

_____

4. Which number is 300 less than 900?

_____

5. What is 200 more than 500?

_____

6. What is 80 subtract 40?

_____

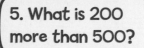
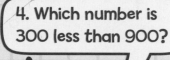

17

Rounding numbers

Learning objective: To round 2-digit and 3-digit numbers and use the results.

We round numbers to make them easier to work with.
It is useful for estimating approximate, or rough, answers.

Rounding to the nearest 10
Look at the units digit.
Round down if the number is less than 5.
Round up if the number is 5 or more.

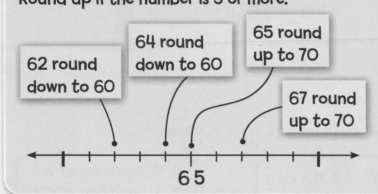

Rounding to the nearest 100
Look at the tens digit.
Round down if the number is less than 50.
Round up if the number is 50 or more.

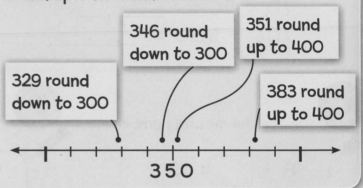

A Round these to the nearest 10.

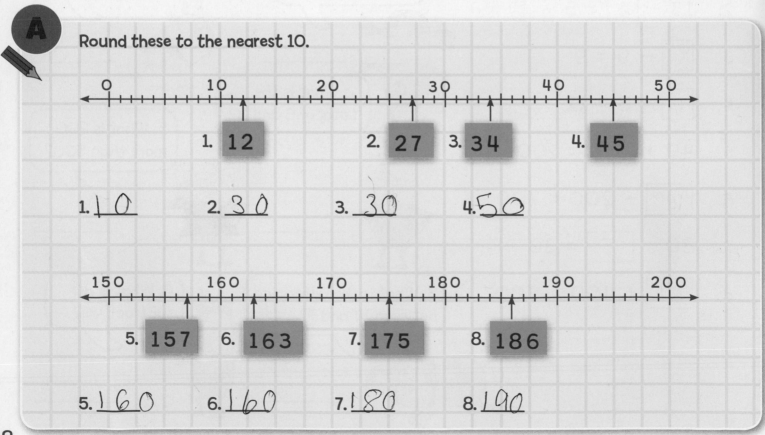

1. 12   2. 27   3. 34   4. 45

1. 10   2. 30   3. 30   4. 50

5. 157   6. 163   7. 175   8. 186

5. 160   6. 160   7. 180   8. 190

B Round these to the nearest 100.

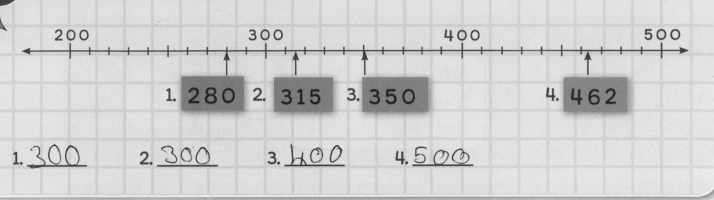

1. 300   2. 300   3. 400   4. 500

We can round numbers to find approximate answers.

Round to the nearest 10	Round to the nearest 100
24 + 67	481 - 176
20 + 70 = 90	500 - 200 = 300

C Round to the nearest 10 and find an approximate answer.

1. 35 + 28
    40 + 30 = 70

2. 97 − 51
    100 − 50 = 50

3. 82 − 44
    80 − 40 = 40

4. 146 + 43
    150 + 40 = 190

Round to the nearest 100 and find an approximate answer.

5. 520 + 175
    500 + 200 = 700

6. 842 − 305
    800 − 300 = 500

7. 651 + 235
    700 + 200 = 900

8. 793 − 619
    800 − 600 = 200

Mentul addition

Break numbers up so that you can add them in your head.

What is 34 add 5?

34 + 5 =
30 + 4 + 5 =
30 + 4 + 5 = 39

Add the ones and then add this to the tens.

Add together 23 and 40.

23 + 40 =
20 + 3 + 40 =
20 + 40 + 3 = 63

Add the tens and then add on the ones.

A

Add the ones then add the tens and write the answer.

1. 63 + 4 = 67
2. 51 + 6 = 57
3. 32 + 3 = 35

4. 22 + 7 = 29
5. 94 + 4 = 98
6. 73 + 5 = 78

B

Add the tens then the ones and write the answer.

1. 56 + 20 = 76
2. 38 + 40 = 78
3. 52 + 30 = 82

4. 23 + 20 = 43
5. 11 + 70 = 81
6. 29 + 60 = 89

C

Join the pairs of sums with the same total.

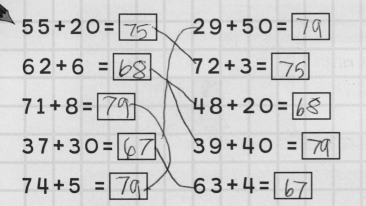

55 + 20 = 75

29 + 50 = 79

62 + 6 = 68

72 + 3 = 75

71 + 8 = 79

48 + 20 = 68

37 + 30 = 67

39 + 40 = 79

74 + 5 = 79

63 + 4 = 67

D

Read the first statement then work out the questions in your head.

My mother is 34.

1. My aunt is 3 years older than my mother. How old is my aunt?

37

2. My father is 5 years older than my aunt. How old is my father?

42

3. My grandmother was 20 when my mother was born. How old is my grandmother?

54

4. My grandfather is 30 years older than my mother. How old is my grandfather?

64

5. My uncle is 4 years older than my father. How old is my uncle?

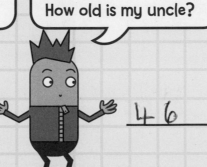

46

6. My great-grandmother is 50 years older than my mother. How old is my great-grandmother?

84

Mental subtraction

Learning objective: To mentally subtract 1- and 2-digit numbers.

Break up numbers so that you can subtract them in your head.

What is 37 subtract 5?

$37 - 5 =$

$30 + 7 - 5 =$

$30 + 7 - 5 = 32$

Subtract the ones and then add this to the tens.

Take away 30 from 54.

$54 - 30 =$

$50 + 4 - 30 =$

$50 - 30 = 20 + 4 = 24$

Subtract the tens and then add on the ones.

A

Break up these numbers to subtract them in your head.

1. $46 - 4 =$ <u>40 + 4 = 36 30</u>   5. $93 - 30 =$ _____

2. $87 - 3 =$ <u>84</u>   6. $52 - 40 =$ _____

3. $29 - 6 =$ <u>23</u>   7. $72 - 30 =$ _____

4. $78 - 50 =$ _____   8. $65 - 3 =$ _____

DEFINITION

find the difference Another way of saying 'subtract' or 'take away'.

B

Find the difference between each pair of numbers.

1. 98   3   _____   4. 82   40   _____

2. 5   57   _____   5. 20   44   _____

3. 3   76   _____   6. 50   91   _____

C

Complete each chart to show the numbers coming out of each subtraction machine.

1.   IN   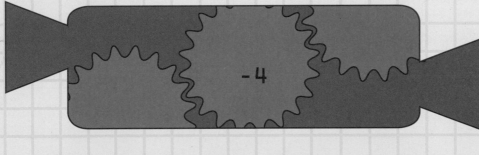   -4   OUT

IN	56	78	27	49	15	64
OUT	52					

2.   IN   -30   OUT

IN	65	91	42	77	59	83
OUT	35					

23

Decimals

Learning objective: To use and understand tenths.

A decimal point is used to separate whole numbers from fractions. The digit after the decimal point shows the number of tenths.

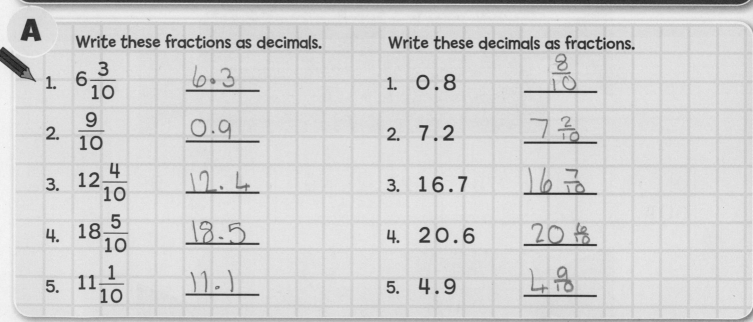

Tenths break up a whole number into 10 equal parts.

$$\frac{1}{10} = 0.1 \qquad \frac{2}{10} = 0.2 \qquad \frac{3}{10} = 0.3$$

Example

15.7

Tens   Units   Tenths

$$10 \; + \; 5 \; + \; \frac{7}{10} \; = \; 15.7$$

15.7

15   16

A

Write these fractions as decimals.

1. $6\frac{3}{10}$ 6.3

2. $\frac{9}{10}$ 0.9

3. $12\frac{4}{10}$ 12.4

4. $18\frac{5}{10}$ 18.5

5. $11\frac{1}{10}$ 11.1

Write these decimals as fractions.

1. 0.8 $\frac{8}{10}$

2. 7.2 $7\frac{2}{10}$

3. 16.7 $16\frac{7}{10}$

4. 20.6 $20\frac{6}{10}$

5. 4.9 $4\frac{9}{10}$

B

Write the value of the digit 2 in each number. Choose from 20, 2 or $\frac{2}{10}$.

1. 12.4   Units   2. 25.5   Tens   3. 16.2   Tenths

4. 3.2   Tenths   5. 0.2   Tenths   6. 42.1   Units

24

DEFINITION

decimal point A point that separates whole numbers from decimal numbers.

C

Look at these number lines and write the decimal number above each arrow.

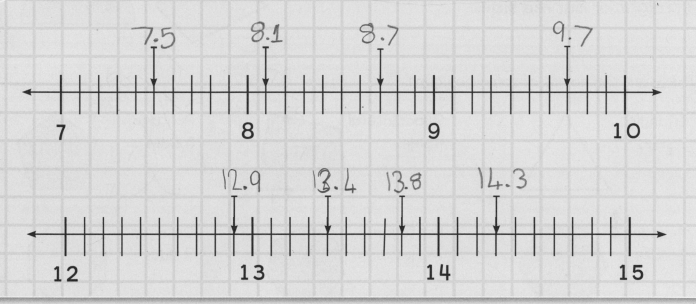

7.5   8.1   8.7   9.7

7   8   9   10

12.9   13.4   13.8   14.3

12   13   14   15

D

Write $<$ or $>$ between these numbers. Use the number lines above to help.

1. 7.6 ___>___ 7.3

2. 8.9 ___<___ 9.8

3. 13.4 ___>___ 12.4

4. 7.5 ___<___ 9.1

5. $9\frac{2}{10}$ ___>___ $7\frac{2}{10}$

6. $13\frac{9}{10}$ ___>___ $13\frac{8}{10}$

7. $8\frac{1}{10}$ ___<___ $9\frac{3}{10}$

8. $12\frac{4}{10}$ ___<___ $14\frac{2}{10}$

Look back at page 10 to find out what $<$ and $>$ mean.

25

2-D shapes

Learning objective: To name, draw and describe 2-D shapes.

2-D shapes are flat shapes. They can have straight or curved sides.

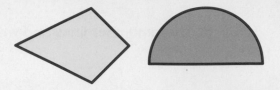

These are the names of some polygons.

Triangle 3 sides	Quadrilateral 4 sides 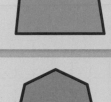	Pentagon 5 sides 
Hexagon 6 sides	Heptagon 7 sides 	Octagon 8 sides 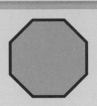

A

Write the name for each shape. Count the number of sides to help find the shape name.

1. _____

2. _____

3. _____

4.  _____

5. 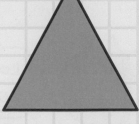 _____

6. 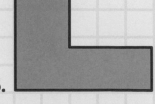 _____

B Write the name of the shapes in each set and the odd one out.

1. These shapes are _____. The odd one out is a _____.

2. These shapes are _____. The odd one out is a _____.

3. These shapes are _____. The odd one out is a _____.

C A pentomino is made from joining five squares. Here are two examples.

Make other pentominoes from five squares. How many can you find?

What shapes are they?

27

Equivalent fractions

Learning objective: To use diagrams to identify equivalent fractions.

Some fractions are equivalent. This means they look different but have the same value.

These are all equivalent to $\frac{1}{2}$:

$\frac{1}{2}$

$\frac{2}{4}$

$\frac{3}{6}$

$\frac{4}{8}$

A

Circle the rectangle that shows an equivalent fraction to each of the following numbers, then fill in the answer.

1. $\dfrac{1}{2}$ (a)   (b)   (c)   (d)

$\dfrac{1}{2} = \dfrac{\quad}{\quad}$

2. $\dfrac{1}{4}$ (a)   (b)   (c)   (d)

$\dfrac{1}{4} = \dfrac{\quad}{\quad}$

3. $\dfrac{1}{3}$ (a)   (b)   (c)   (d)

$\dfrac{1}{3} = \dfrac{\quad}{\quad}$

4. $\dfrac{1}{5}$ (a)   (b)   (c)   (d)

$\dfrac{1}{5} = \dfrac{\quad}{\quad}$

equivalent fractions These are equal fractions. Example: $\frac{1}{2} = \frac{2}{4}$

B

Look at the fractions that are shaded. Write each fraction in two ways.

1. $\dfrac{}{} = \dfrac{}{}$

2. $\dfrac{}{} = \dfrac{}{}$

3. $\dfrac{}{} = \dfrac{}{}$

C

Here are four members of the half family.

$$\frac{4}{8} \qquad \frac{6}{12} \qquad \frac{7}{14} \qquad \frac{10}{20}$$

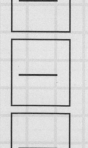

Write five members of each of these fraction families.

1. $\dfrac{1}{3}$ $\dfrac{}{}$ $\dfrac{}{}$ $\dfrac{}{}$ $\dfrac{}{}$ $\dfrac{}{}$

2. $\dfrac{1}{4}$ $\dfrac{}{}$ $\dfrac{}{}$ $\dfrac{}{}$ $\dfrac{}{}$ $\dfrac{}{}$

3. $\dfrac{1}{5}$ $\dfrac{}{}$ $\dfrac{}{}$ $\dfrac{}{}$ $\dfrac{}{}$ $\dfrac{}{}$

Measuring length

Learning objective: To read, estimate, measure and record using centimetres

A ruler is a useful tool for measuring smaller lengths.

This shows a **centimetre** ruler.

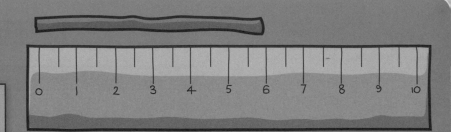

- Each division is 1 centimetre in length.
- Each small division between the centimetres is half a centimetre.
- The length of the stick is 6 centimetres, or 6cm.

DEFINITION

estimate An estimate is a rough answer, without measuring.

A

Look at the ruler above and estimate the length of each line.
Write your estimate in centimetres.

1. estimate: _____cm
_____

2. estimate: _____cm
_____

3. estimate: _____cm
_____

4. estimate: _____cm
_____

5. estimate: _____cm
_____

6. estimate: _____cm
_____

Take your best guess!

B

Use a ruler and measure the exact length of each line in Section A. Write each length in centimetres.

1. length: _____cm

2. length: _____cm

3. length: _____cm

4. length: _____cm

5. length: _____cm

6. length: _____cm

C

Measure each item and write the lengths.

1. cotton: _____cm

2. needle: _____cm

3. paperclip: _____cm

4. zip: _____cm

5. screwdriver: _____ cm

6. screw: _____cm

7. nail: _____cm

8. toothbrush: _____cm

Multiplication facts

Learning objective: To know the multiplication facts up to 10 x 10.

Use the multiplication facts you already know to help learn other facts.

Example

3 x 5 = 15	8 x 2 = 16	10 x 6 = 60
3 x 6 is 3 more → 18	8 x 4 is double 16 → 32	9 x 6 is 6 less → 54

Remember 3 x 7 gives the same answer as 7 x 3.

It's easy when you know the facts!

A   Answer these.

1. 6 x 4 = _____

2. 3 x 7 = _____

3. 9 x 3 = _____

4. 5 x 9 = _____

5. 6 x 5 = _____

6. 7 x 8 = _____

DEFINITION

multiplication fact It is true that 3 x 5 = 15. This is a multiplication fact.

B

Write the answers for each of these.

1. 5 x 7 = _____

   6 x 7 = _____

2. 5 x 8 = _____

   6 x 8 = _____

3. 10 x 6 = _____

   9 x 6 = _____

4. 10 x 8 = _____

   9 x 8 = _____

5. 3 x 3 = _____

   6 x 3 = _____

6. 2 x 7 = _____

   4 x 7 = _____

7. 4 x 4 = _____

   8 x 4 = _____

8. 2 x 9 = _____

   4 x 9 = _____

C

Read and answer these.

1. Julie buys 4 packs of plates. What is the total number of plates she will have? _____

2. Sam buys 3 packs of straws. How many straws does he have in total? _____

3. Owen wants 12 glasses. How many packs of glasses will he need to buy? _____

4. Owen also wants 12 plates. How many packs of plates will he need to buy? _____

5. Sabina wants 20 glasses. How many packs of glasses will she need to buy? _____

6. Tess wants 20 straws. How many packs of straws does she need to buy? _____

Now see if you can complete this tricky challenge!

D

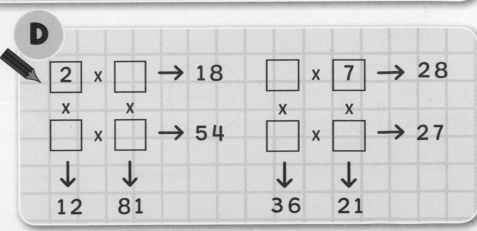

33

Time

Learning objective: To read the time to the nearest 5 minutes.

There are 60 minutes in 1 hour. It takes 5 minutes for the minute hand to move from one marker to the next.

This shows the hour. It is past 3 o'clock.

I wonder how long it will take you to complete this page?

This shows the number of minutes past the hour. It is 40 minutes past 3 or 3.40.

A Write these times.

1. _____

2. _____

3. _____

4. _____

5. _____

6. _____

7. _____

8. _____

B

Read these time problems. Write the answers.

1. A TV programme starts at 6.15 and lasts for half an hour.
   What time will it end? _____

2. Nathan gets up at 7 o'clock and leaves for school an hour later.
   What time does he leave for school? _____

3. A boat leaves at 10 past 1 and returns at half-past one.
   How long was the boat at sea? _____

4. A cake takes 25 minutes to bake. It was put in the oven at 4 o'clock.
   When will it be ready? _____

5. Gemma is playing at the park. It is quarter to 12. She has to go home at 12.30.
   How much longer does she have to play? _____

C

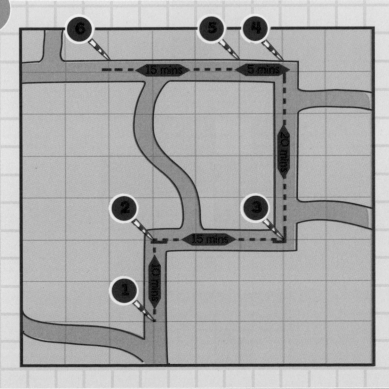

Look at the map showing the length of time a bus takes between each stop. Complete this bus timetable. Work out the time the bus will be at each stop.

Bus Stop	Time
1	9.05
2	
3	
4	
5	
6	

Measuring area

To find the area of a shape you can draw it on a square grid and count the squares.

The side of each small square on this grid is 1cm.

This shape has an area of 12 square centimetres.

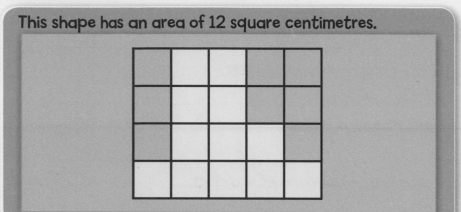

A Count the squares and write the area of each shape.

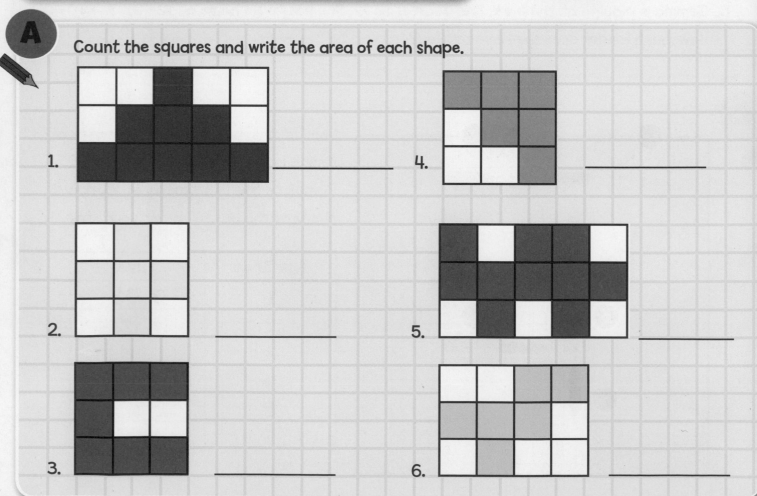

1. _____

2. _____

3. _____

4. _____

5. _____

6. _____

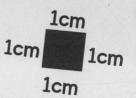
B

This plan shows the gardens of a hotel. Each square shows 1 square metre of ground. Count the squares and write the area for each section.

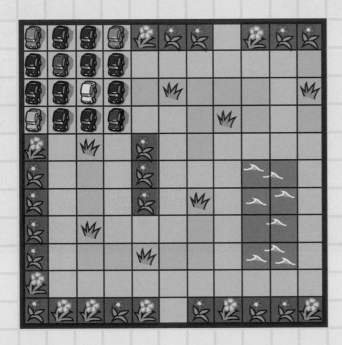

1. Area of swimming pool = _____ square metres

2. Area of paths = _____ square metres

3. Area of car park = _____ square metres

4. Area of grass = _____ square metres

5. Area of flower border = _____ square metres

C

A gardener is planning a path using 8 slabs. Each slab is 1 square metre. Here are two designs using 8 squares. Draw 3 more path designs using 8 squares.

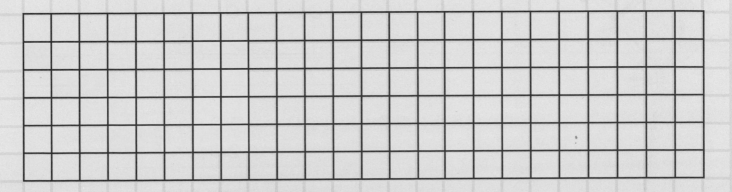

Written addition

Learning objective: To add 2- and 3-digit numbers.

When you can't work out an addition in your head, try a written method.

Example 1

46 + 25 → 40 + 6 + 20 + 5 = 60 + 11 = 71

Example 2

138 + 54

100 + 30 + 8
+   50 + 4
100 + 80 + 12 → 100 + 80 + 12 = 192

With this short method, add the ones, tens and then the hundreds.

```
  138
+  54
 ----
  192
    1
```

Make sure you line up the digits correctly.

A

Add these and write the answers.

1. 267 + 18 → 200 + 60 + 7
              +   10 + 8
              _____
                 +   +   = _____

2. 109 + 79 → 100 + 0   + 9
              +   70 + 9
              _____
                 +   +   = _____

3. 254 + 27 → 200 + 50 + 4
              +   20 + 7
              _____
                 +   +   = _____

B

Now answer these. Use paper for your working out.

1. 143
   + 37

2. 215
   + 29

3. 238
   + 58

4. 126
   + 35

C

Read and answer these. Use paper for your working out.

1. What is 15 more than 78? _____

2. Add 57 and 26. _____

3. What is the total of 33 and 39? _____

4. Increase 124 by 47. _____

5. Total 265 and 29. _____

6. What is 46 added to 205? _____

D

Read and answer these problems. Use paper for your working out.

1. A truck driver travels 53 kilometres in the morning and 37 kilometres in the afternoon.
   How far does the truck travel in total? _____

2. A market stall sells 28 bottles of mango juice and 39 bottles of orange juice.
   What is the total number of bottles sold? _____

3. A farmer has 44 chickens and 17 ducks.
   How many chickens and ducks are there altogether? _____

4. A postman has 149 letters and 36 parcels.
   How many items altogether are there to deliver? _____

5. Jamal has read 108 pages of his reading book and there are 52 pages left.
   How many pages in total are there in Jamal's reading book? _____

6. Julie is 136 centimetres tall and her dad is 38 centimetres taller than she is.
   How tall is Julie's dad? _____

Written subtraction

Learning objective: To subtract 2-digit numbers.

When you can't work out a subtraction in your head, try a written method.

Look at these two methods.

53 - 38

Break up 53 into 40 and 13:

$$
\begin{array}{r}
{}^4\ {}^{13} \\
\not5\ 3 \\
-\ 3\ 8 \\
\hline
1\ 5 \\
\hline
\end{array}
$$

13 – 8 = 5   40 – 30 = 10

Counting on to find the difference:

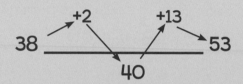

Count on from 38 to 40 and then to 53.

$$2\ +\ 13\ =\ 15$$

So the difference between 38 and 53 is 15.

A

Answer these.

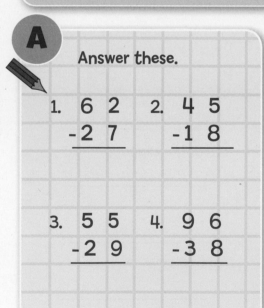

1. 6 2   2. 4 5
   -2 7   -1 8

3. 5 5   4. 9 6
   -2 9   -3 8

B

Count on to find the difference between these numbers.

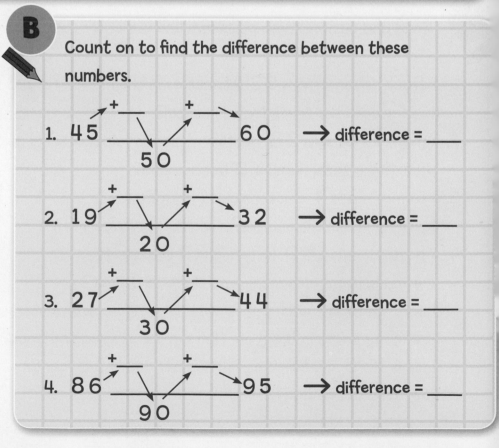

1. 45 _____ 60   → difference = ____
        50

2. 19 _____ 32   → difference = ____
        20

3. 27 _____ 44   → difference = ____
        30

4. 86 _____ 95   → difference = ____
        90

C Read and answer these.

1. What is the difference between 28 and 48? _____

2. Subtract 16 from 43. _____

3. What number is 34 less than 52? _____

4. What is 80 take away 29? _____

5. How much greater is 91 than 76? _____

6. What is 66 subtract 37? _____

D

Now try this cool number puzzle!

a) 2		b)	c)	
2	d)			e)
f)		g)	h)	
	i)			j)

The puzzle works like a crossword. Solve the clues and write one digit in each space. Question (a) down has been done for you.

Clues

Across	Down
a) 53 – 26	a) 44 – 22
c) 60 – 21	b) 31 – 16
d) 52 – 17	c) 59 – 23
f) 65 – 24	d) 42 – 11
h) 41 – 26	e) 60 – 15
i) 58 – 11	f) 72 – 26
j) 57 – 49	g) 64 – 27
	h) 36 – 18

41

Symmetry

Learning objective: To recognize and draw shapes with reflective symmetry.

A line of symmetry is like a mirror line.
One half of the shape looks like the reflection of the other half.

Look at these lines of symmetry.

A

Draw a line down the centre of each picture then fill in the table.

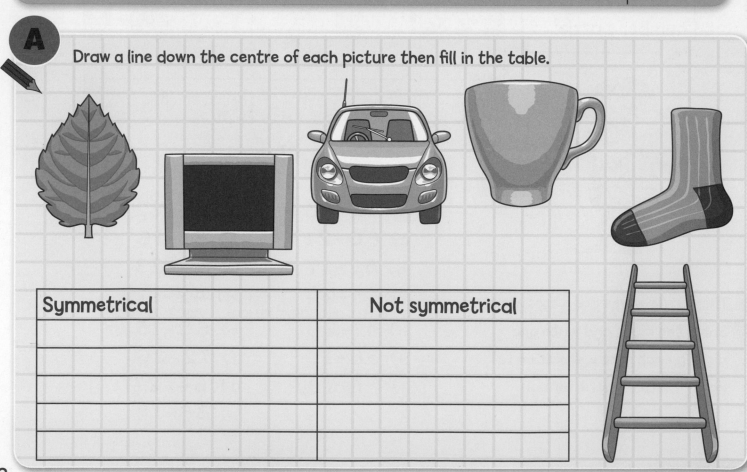

Symmetrical	Not symmetrical

DEFINITION

symmetry When two parts of a shape are exactly the same, as though one was the reflection of the other in a mirror.

B

Complete these drawings to make symmetrical shapes.

1.

2.

3.

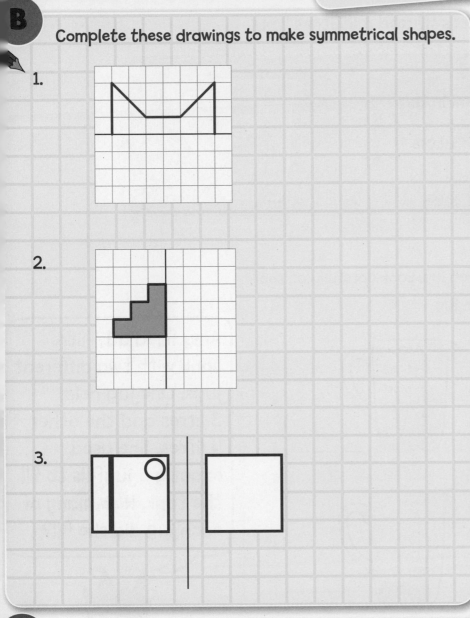

Now try to work out what are the mystery symmetry words below! Make up more mystery words of your own.

DECK, CODE, HOOD

V ⊢⁄⅂, ⅂⊂ V, ⊢⅂ ᴎ

C

Some letters of the alphabet and some numbers are symmetrical. Complete each of these letters and numbers.

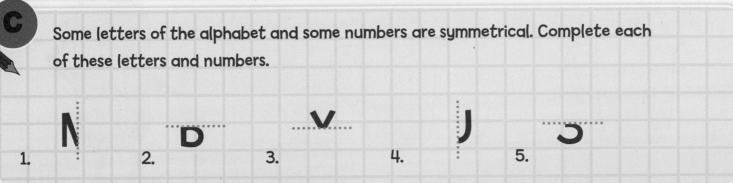

1.   M   2.   D   3.   V   4.   J   5.   Ɔ

43

Measuring Capacity

Learning objective: To read scales and use litres and millilitres.

Metric units of capacity are litres (l) and millilitres (ml).

There are 1000ml in 1l.

1000 millilitres = 1 litre

A

Write the amount shown in each jug. Look carefully at the units of measurement for each jug.

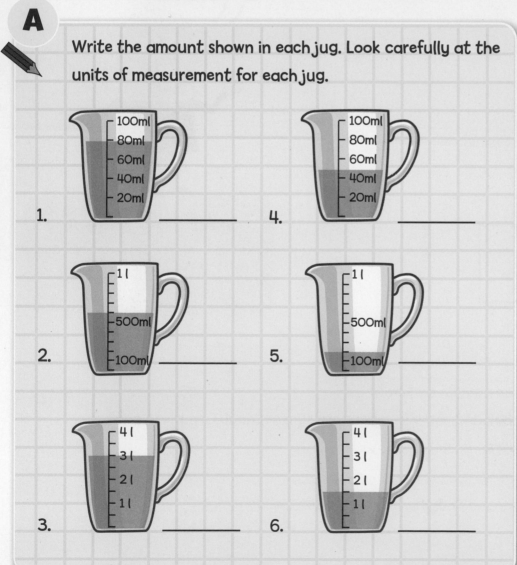

1. _____

4. _____

2. _____

5. _____

3. _____

6. _____

Amy filled a 17-litre tank with two different jugs. One jug held 3 litres and the other 4 litres. She used exactly 5 jugfuls to fill the tank. How many of each jug did she fill?

44

DEFINITION

capacity This is how much something holds.

B

Each of these containers holds a different amount.

$\frac{1}{4}$ litre $\frac{1}{2}$ litre   1 litre   2 litre

How many of each of these containers would you need to fill a 1 litre jug?

1. __ cups = 1 litre   2. __ glasses = 1 litre   3. __ milk bottle = 1 litre

How many of each of these containers would you need to make 2 litres?

4. __ milk bottles = 2 litres   5.  __ water bottle = 2 litres

C

Answer these.

1. How many 500ml bottles will fill a 1 litre jug? _____
2. How many 100ml large spoons will fill a 1 litre jug? _____
3. How many 250ml cups will fill a 1 litre jug? _____
4. How many 5ml teaspoons will fill a 100ml large spoon? _____
5. How many 500ml bottles will fill a 2 litre jug? _____
6. How many 100ml large spoons will fill a 500ml water bottle? _____

45

Multiplication

Learning objective: To multiply a 2-digit number by a 1-digit number.

There are different methods for multiplying numbers.

Example 1

What is 38 multiplied by 5?

$38 \times 5 \rightarrow$
$30 \times 5 = 150$
$8 \times 5 = \underline{\quad 40} +$
$38 \times 5 = \underline{190}$

Example 2

What is 24 multiplied by 6?

$\times$	20	4
6	120	24

$\rightarrow 120 + 24 = \mathbf{144}$

A Complete these multiplications.

1. $\mathbf{14 \times 4} \rightarrow$
$10 \times 4 =$
$4 \times 4 = \underline{\quad\quad} +$
$14 \times 4 = \underline{\quad\quad\quad}$

2. $\mathbf{25 \times 9} \rightarrow$
$20 \times 9 =$
$5 \times 9 = \underline{\quad\quad} +$
$25 \times 9 = \underline{\quad\quad\quad}$

3. $\mathbf{37 \times 6} \rightarrow$
$30 \times 6 =$
$7 \times 6 = \underline{\quad\quad} +$
$37 \times 6 = \underline{\quad\quad\quad}$

4. $\mathbf{58 \times 3} \rightarrow$
$50 \times 3 =$
$8 \times 3 = \underline{\quad\quad} +$
$58 \times 3 = \underline{\quad\quad\quad}$

B Complete these multiplications using a grid.

1. $\mathbf{76 \times 2} = \underline{\quad\quad}$

$\times$	70	6
2		

$\rightarrow \underline{\quad\quad\quad}$

2. $\mathbf{23 \times 8} = \underline{\quad\quad}$

$\times$	20	3
8		

$\rightarrow \underline{\quad\quad\quad}$

3. $\mathbf{39 \times 4} = \underline{\quad\quad}$

$\times$	30	9
4		

$\rightarrow \underline{\quad\quad\quad}$

4. $\mathbf{37 \times 5} = \underline{\quad\quad}$

$\times$	30	7
5		

$\rightarrow \underline{\quad\quad\quad}$

C

Answer these. Choose a method for working out each answer. Use paper for your working out.

1. 86 x 2 = _____
2. 47 x 3 = _____
3. 19 x 9 = _____

4. 23 x 8 = _____
5. 34 x 6 = _____
6. 28 x 5 = _____

D

Read and answer these problems.

1. A bus holds 48 passengers. How many people will 4 buses hold?

   _____

2. Mr Duke travels 19 kilometres each day to and from work. He works 5 days a week. How far does he travel altogether in a week?

   _____

3. A market stall has 6 crates of melons. There are 35 melons in a crate. How many melons are there in total?

   _____

4. A farmer fills 4 trays of eggs. Each tray holds 36 eggs. How many eggs does the farmer have?

   _____

5. The battery in a mobile phone lasts 7 days. How many hours does the battery last?

   _____

6. A dog eats 59 dog biscuits per day. How many will it eat in 3 days?

   _____

Look for the multiplication sum in each of these problems.

Use the multiplication facts that you know.

Measuring perimeter

Learning objective: To measure the perimeter of rectangles.

The perimeter of a shape is the distance all around the edge.

This tile has a perimeter of 3cm + 3cm + 5cm + 5cm = 16cm

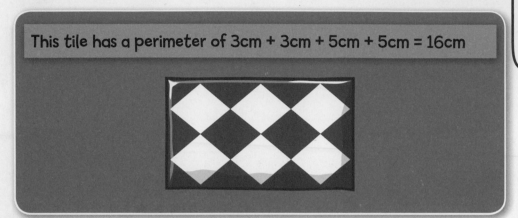

Use a ruler to check these measurements.

A

Calculate the distance round each of these shapes. Write the perimeters in metres.

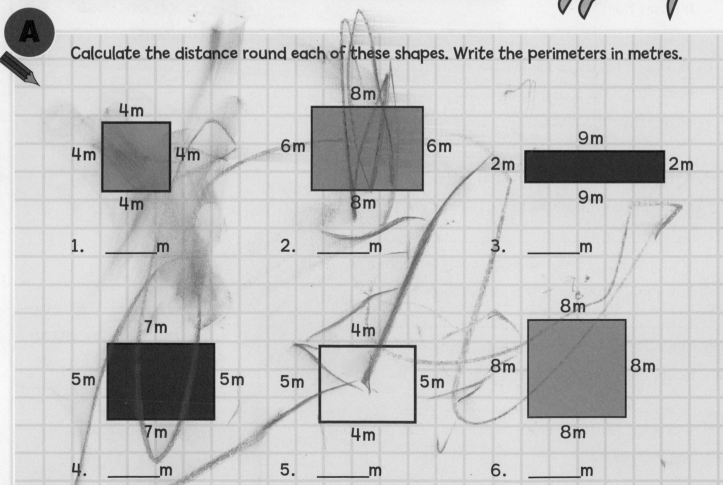

4m
4m   4m
4m

1. _____m

8m
6m   6m
8m

2. _____m

9m
2m   2m
9m

3. _____m

7m
5m   5m
7m

4. _____m

4m
5m   5m
4m

5. _____m

8m
8m   8m
8m

6. _____m

B

Use a ruler to measure the sides of each rectangle. Write the length, height and perimeter for these in centimetres.

1.

Length = _____cm

Height = _____cm

Perimeter = _____cm

2.

Length = _____cm

Height = _____cm

Perimeter = _____cm

3.

Length = _____cm

Height = _____cm

Perimeter = _____cm

4.

Length = _____cm

Height = _____cm

Perimeter = _____cm

5.

Length = _____cm

Height = _____cm

Perimeter = _____cm

6.

Length = _____cm

Height = _____cm

Perimeter = _____cm

C

Complete this chart. Write the length and height of each rectangle and calculate the perimeter.

1.
6m
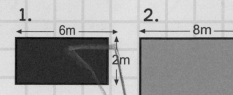
2m

2.
8m
4m

3.
5m

5m

4.
7m
9m

5.
11m
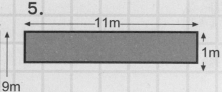
1m

Rectangle	length	add	height	Multiply total by 2		Perimeter
1	m	+	m	=	m → x 2	m
2	m	+	m	=	m → x 2	m
3	m	+	m	=	m → x 2	m
4	m	+	m	=	m → x 2	m
5	m	+	m	=	m → x 2	m

Angles

Learning objective: To use degrees to measure angles.

We use degrees (°) to measure angles.

A $\frac{1}{4}$ turn is also called a right angle.
There are 90 degrees (90°) in a right angle.

A complete turn is the same as four right angles, or 360°.

A straight line is 180°.

A

1. Take a piece of scrap paper.
2. Fold it to make a straight line.
3. Fold it again to make a right angle.

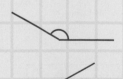

An estimate is your best guess.

B

Estimate the size in degrees of each of these angles.

Use your folded right angle to help. (You can fold 90° in half again to make 45°.)

1. 2. 3. 4.

5. 6. 7. 8.

Complete the table to show your estimates.

Angle	1.	2.	3.	4.	5.	6.	7.	8.
Estimated size (°)								

B

Draw the right angles on these shapes. The first one has been done for you.

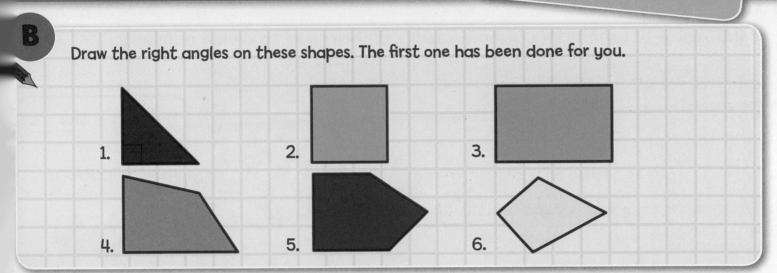

1.   2.   3.

4.   5.   6.

D

Look at these 6 angles. Estimate the size of each angle.

Now write them in order of size, starting with the smallest: __ __ __ __ __ __

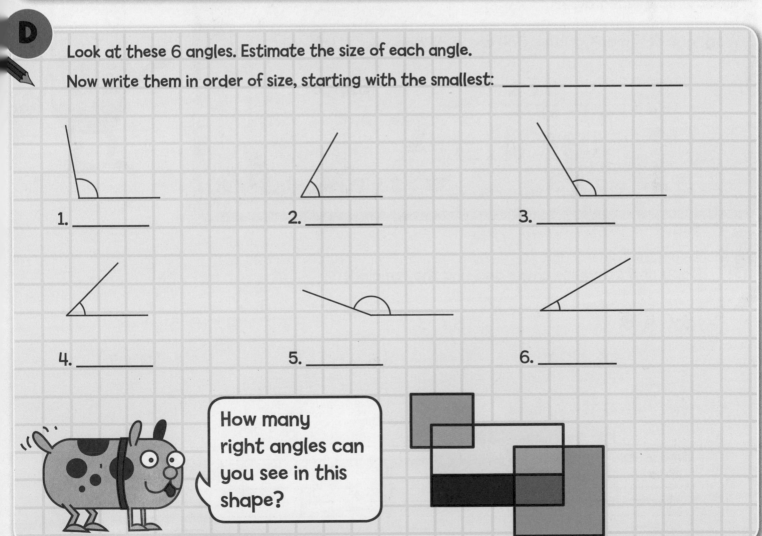

1. _____   2. _____   3. _____

4. _____   5. _____   6. _____

How many right angles can you see in this shape?

51

Division

If you know your multiplication facts it can help you to divide numbers.

Look at the trio 6, 3 and 18:

$6 \times 3 = 18$ $3 \times 6 = 18$

$18 \div 3 = 6$ $18 \div 6 = 3$

Division is the opposite of multiplication.

If a number cannot be divided exactly it leaves a remainder.

Example

What is 35 divided by 4?

Work out how many groups of 4 are in 35 and what is left over:

$$\begin{array}{r} 8 \text{ r } 3 \\ 4\overline{)35} \\ -32 \quad (4 \times 8) \\ \hline 3 \end{array}$$

Answer

$35 \div 4 = 8$ remainder 3

A

Copy and complete these and find the remainders.

1. $5\overline{)48}$ r___

    ___ (5 x 9)

    ___

2. $6\overline{)37}$ r___

    ___ (6 x 6)

    ___

3. $9\overline{)65}$ r___

    ___ (9 x 7)

    ___

4. $3\overline{)26}$ r___

    ___ (__ x __)

    ___

5. $7\overline{)40}$ r___

    ___ (__ x __)

    ___

6. $8\overline{)52}$ r___

    ___ (__ x __)

    ___

DEFINITION

division This is like sharing an amount of something.

B Complete these.

1. ___ ÷ 4 = 7

2. 18 ÷ ___ = 2

3. ___ x 6 = 36

4. 40 ÷ 5 = ___

5. 8 x ___ = 24

6. ___ x 7 = 21

7. 54 ÷ ___ = 9

8. 6 x ___ = 48

9. 63 ÷ 9 = ___

10. ___ ÷ 4 = 8

I'm thinking of a number. It is less than 100 and if I divide it by 2, 3, 4, 5, 6 or 10 it leaves a remainder of 1. What is my number?

C Mrs Folkes is grouping her class into teams. She has 35 pupils in her class.

Read and answer these questions:

1. The School Maths Quiz has 3 pupils in each team. How many quiz teams can be made from Mrs Folkes' class? _____

2. Helper Teams have 8 children to help around the school. Any children left over will join children from another class. How many children will be left over in Mrs Folkes' class? _____

3. Mrs Folkes is dividing her class into sports teams. Complete this chart.

Sport	Number of players in each team	Total number of teams	Number of students left over
Doubles Tennis	2 players per team	17 teams	1 left over
400m Relay Race	4 players per team	8 teams	
Basketball	5 players per team		0 left over
Volleyball	6 players per team		
Netball	7 players per team		

Fractions of quantities

Learning objective: To find fractions of numbers and quantities.

Remember that fractions have a numerator and a denominator.

$$\text{denominator} \rightarrow \frac{3 \leftarrow \text{numerator}}{4}$$

Example 1

What is $\frac{1}{5}$ of 40?

When the numerator is 1, just divide by the denominator.

$$\frac{1}{5} \text{ of } 40 = 40 \div 5 = 8$$

Example 2

What is $\frac{3}{5}$ of 40?

When the numerator is more than 1, divide by the denominator then multiply by the numerator.

$$\frac{1}{5} \text{ of } 40 = 8$$

$$\frac{3}{5} = \frac{1}{5} \times 3 \left(\frac{1}{5} + \frac{1}{5} + \frac{1}{5} \right)$$

so, $\frac{3}{5}$ of 40 = 8 x 3 = 24

A

Use the dots to work out these fractions.

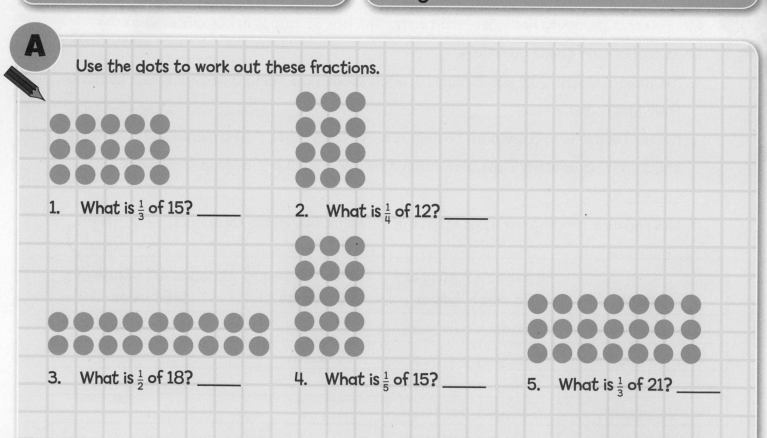

1. What is $\frac{1}{3}$ of 15? _____

2. What is $\frac{1}{4}$ of 12? _____

3. What is $\frac{1}{2}$ of 18? _____

4. What is $\frac{1}{5}$ of 15? _____

5. What is $\frac{1}{3}$ of 21? _____

B

There are 24 balloons of different shapes and colours in a pack. How many of each type of balloon are there?

$\frac{1}{2}$ are red: _____ red balloons

$\frac{1}{6}$ are yellow: _____ yellow balloons

$\frac{1}{3}$ are blue: _____ blue balloons

$\frac{1}{4}$ are large balloons: _____ large balloons

$\frac{1}{8}$ are long balloons: _____ long balloons

24 ASSORTED BALLOONS

David has 64 sweets. He gives $\frac{3}{4}$ to his classmates. How many does he have left?

C

Answer each pair of questions

1. $\frac{1}{5}$ of 35 = _____
   $\frac{2}{5}$ of 35 = _____

2. $\frac{1}{4}$ of 40 = _____
   $\frac{3}{4}$ of 40 = _____

3. $\frac{1}{7}$ of 21 = _____
   $\frac{5}{7}$ of 21 = _____

4. $\frac{1}{9}$ of 18 = _____
   $\frac{8}{9}$ of 18 = _____

5. $\frac{1}{10}$ of 70 = _____
   $\frac{7}{10}$ of 70 = _____

6. $\frac{1}{8}$ of 32 = _____
   $\frac{7}{8}$ of 32 = _____

7. $\frac{1}{3}$ of 33 = _____
   $\frac{2}{3}$ of 33 = _____

8. $\frac{1}{6}$ of 30 = _____
   $\frac{5}{6}$ of 30 = _____

Use multiplication and division facts to solve these.

Measuring weight

We use **kilograms** to measure the weight of heavy objects.
We use **grams** to measure the weight of light objects.

I weigh 80 kilograms.

This salt weighs 500 grams.

1 kilogram (kg) = 1000 grams (g)
$\frac{1}{2}$kg = 500g

A

Write the weight for each of these.

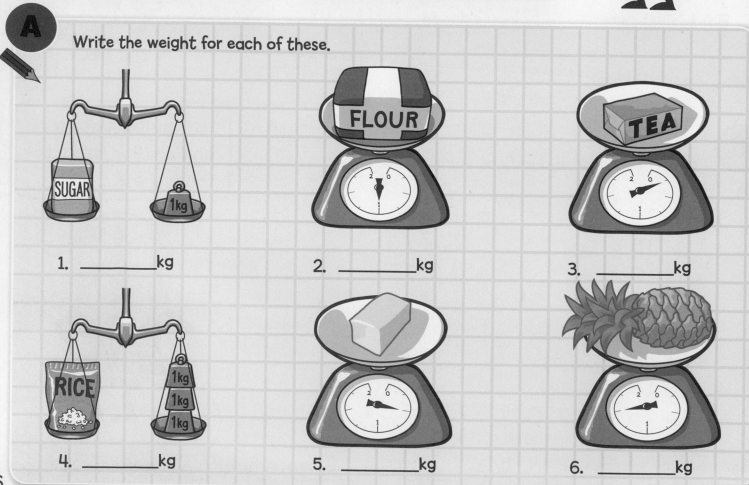

1. _____ kg

2. _____ kg

3. _____ kg

4. _____ kg

5. _____ kg

6. _____ kg

56

B Convert these measures.

1. 2000g = _____ kg

2. 5kg = _____ g

3. 4000g = _____ kg

4. 6kg = _____ g

5. 9kg = _____ g

6. 3000g = _____ kg

These shapes weigh 18kg altogether. If each pyramid weighs 3kg, what is the weight of each cube?

C Write the weight of each bag to the nearest ½kg.

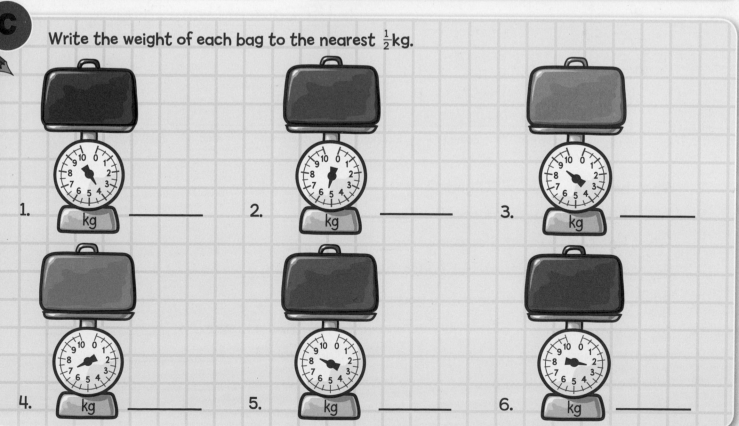

1. kg _____

2. kg _____

3. kg _____

4. kg _____

5. kg _____

6. kg _____

57

Learning objective: To read the data in bar graphs.

Data is information that has been collected.

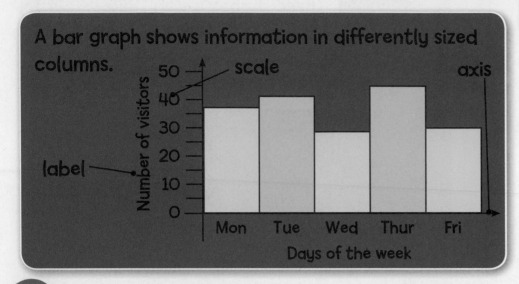

A bar graph shows information in differently sized columns.

scale

axis

Number of visitors

label

Mon Tue Wed Thur Fri

Days of the week

Do you know the names of any other types of graph?

A

Answer these questions about the bar graph.

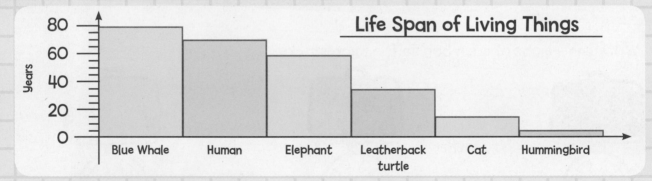

Life Span of Living Things

Years

Blue Whale   Human   Elephant   Leatherback turtle   Cat   Hummingbird

1. What has a life span of 70 years? _____

2. What has the longest life span? _____

3. What has the shortest life span? _____

4. How long might a leatherback turtle live?_____

5. What has a life span of about 15 years? _____

6. How much longer is a blue whale expected to live than a human? _____

7. What is expected to live twenty years more than a cat? _____

8. What creatures are expected to live longer than 50 years? _____
_____

B

This chart shows the favourite fruits of children in Class 3.

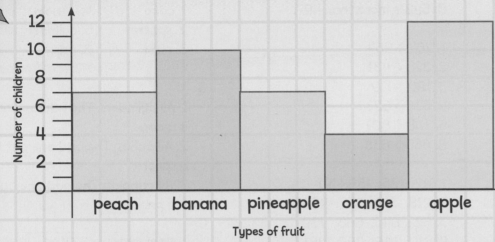

Take the difference between the number of children who liked oranges compared to those who liked peaches. Add that to the number who liked pineapple. That will give the number of people who liked my favourite fruit!

1. How many children chose bananas as their favourite fruit?

_____ children

2. Which type of fruit did 12 children choose as their favourite?

_____

3. Which fruit did the least number of children choose? _____

4. How many children chose peaches as their favourite fruit?

_____ children

5. How many children altogether chose bananas or pineapples?

_____ children

6. How many more children liked apples than bananas?

_____ more children

7. Which two fruits did the same number of children choose?

_____ and _____

8. Which are the two most popular fruits?

_____ and _____

9. How many more children liked bananas than oranges?

_____ more children

Answers

Pages 6-7

A Odd →15, 17, 29, 33, 21
   Even → 24, 20, 32, 22, 16, 38, 30

B Check odd numbers are circled
   and even numbers are underlined.
   1. 11   2. 12   3. 17   4. 16   5. 21

C
   1. 36, 38   2. 27, 29
   3. 52, 54   4. 33, 35

Challenge: 234,456,789 is odd.

Pages 8-9

A
   1. 300 + 90 + 8
   2. 200 + 10 + 7
   3. 400 + 50 + 2
   4. 600 + 80 + 3
   5. 100 + 60 + 5
   6. 700 + 0 + 9

B
   1. nine hundred and forty-one
   2. 326
   3. five hundred and thirty-four
   4. eight hundred and seventy
   5. 219
   6. 650

C
   1. 83
   2. 545
   3. 911
   4. 628
   5. 704
   6. 367

Pages 10-11

A
   1. 147 is less than 152.
   2. 476 is less than 479.
   3. 753 is more than 735.
   4. 521 is more than 381.
   5. 190 is less than 390.
   6. 214 is less than 244.
   7. 586 is more than 585.
   8. 592 is more than 497.

B
   1. 264 > 254
   2. 328 < 431
   3. 190 > 119
   4. 536 > 523
   5. 708 < 807
   6. 655 > 635

C
   1. 112, 125, 159, 191
   2. 278, 373, 387, 483
   3. 622, 645, 668, 739
   4. 410, 416, 460, 461
   5. 704, 743, 760, 778
   6. 195, 309, 459, 815

Pages 12-13

A
   1. 42, 47   5. 84, 80
   2. 93, 95   6. 479, 469
   3. 43, 40   7. 668, 768
   4. 60, 64   8. 531, 431

B
   1. 85, 145   The rule is +15
   2. 500, 450   The rule is -50
   3. 943, 743   The rule is -100
   4. 619, 419   The rule is -100
   5. 820, 840   The rule is +5
   6. 472, 502   The rule is +10
   7. 113, 103   The rule is -10
   8. 512, 527   The rule is +3

C
   1. 995, 985, 975, 965, 955, 945, 935
   2. 80, 180, 280, 380, 480, 580, 680
   3. 857, 855, 853, 851, 849, 847, 845

Pages 14-15

A
   1. cone   4. cuboid
   2. sphere   5. cylinder
   3. cube   6. prism

B
   1. All cylinders. The odd one out is a cone.
   2. All cubes. The odd one out is a sphere.
   3. All cuboids. The odd one out is a prism.

C

Name of shape	cube	cuboid	prism
Total number of faces	6	6	5
Number of square and rectangle faces	6	6	3
Number of triangular faces	0	0	2

D
   1. never 2. always 3. never
   4. sometimes

Pages 16-17

A
   1. 7 + 8 = 15   15 - 7 = 8
       8 + 7 = 15   15 - 8 = 7
   2. 6 + 6 = 12   12 - 6 = 6
       6 + 6 = 12   12 - 6 = 6
   3. 9 + 5 = 14   14 - 9 = 5
       5 + 9 = 14   14 - 5 = 9
   4. 9 + 7 = 16   16 - 9 = 7
       7 + 9 = 16   16 - 7 = 9

B
   1. 15, 150, 1500
   2. 4, 40, 400
   3. 12, 120, 1200
   4. 2, 20, 200

1. 9   5. 60
2. 8   6. 900
3. 18   7. 50
4. 4   8. 200

1. 90   4. 600
2. 14   5. 700
3. 7   6. 40

Pages 18-19

A

1. 10   5. 160
2. 30   6. 160
3. 30   7. 180
4. 50   8. 190

B

1. 300   2. 300   3. 400   4. 500

C

1. 40+30=70   5. 500+200=700
2. 100-50=50   6. 800-300=500
3. 80-40=40   7. 700+200=900
4. 150+40=190   8. 800-600=200

Pages 20-21

A

1. 67   4. 29
2. 57   5. 98
3. 35   6. 78

B

1. 76   4. 43
2. 78   5. 81
3. 82   6. 89

C

55 + 20 → 72 + 3
71 + 8 → 29 + 50
37 + 30 → 63 + 4
62 + 6 → 48 + 20
74 + 5 → 39 + 40

D

1. 37   4. 64
2. 42   5. 46
3. 54   6. 84

Pages 22-23

A

1. 42   5. 63
2. 84   6. 12
3. 23   7. 42
4. 28   8. 62

B

1. 95   4. 42
2. 52   5. 24
3. 73   6. 41

C

1.
IN	56	78	27	49	15	64
OUT	52	74	23	45	11	60

2.
IN	65	91	42	77	59	83
OUT	35	61	12	47	29	53

Pages 24-25

A

1. 6.3   4. 18.5
2. 0.9   5. 11.1
3. 12.4

1. $\frac{8}{10}$ 4. $20\frac{6}{10}$
2. $7\frac{2}{10}$ 5. $4\frac{9}{10}$
3. $16\frac{7}{10}$

B

1. 2   4. $\frac{2}{10}$
2. 20   5. $\frac{2}{10}$
3. $\frac{2}{10}$ 6. 2

C

7.5   8.1   8.7   9.7
12.9 13.4 13.8 14.3

D

1. >   5. >
2. <   6. >
3. >   7. <
4. <   8. <

Pages 26-27

A

1. quadrilateral, 2. octagon,
3. hexagon, 4. pentagon,
5. triangle, 6. hexagon

B

1. Hexagons - odd one out is a
quadrilateral.
2. Quadrilaterals - odd one out
is a pentagon.
3. Ovals - odd one out is a
circle.

C Check all shapes are
pentominoes.

Pages 28-29

A

1. (d) $\frac{2}{4}$ 2. (a) $\frac{2}{8}$
3. (b) $\frac{3}{9}$ 4. (d) $\frac{2}{10}$

B

1. $\frac{5}{10} = \frac{1}{2}$ 2. $\frac{1}{3} = \frac{2}{6}$
3. $\frac{4}{16} = \frac{1}{4}$

C

Possible answers could be:

$\frac{1}{3} = \frac{2}{6}\ \frac{3}{9}\ \frac{4}{12}\ \frac{5}{15}\ \frac{6}{18}$

$\frac{1}{4} = \frac{2}{8}\ \frac{3}{12}\ \frac{4}{16}\ \frac{5}{20}\ \frac{6}{24}$

$\frac{1}{5} = \frac{2}{10}\ \frac{3}{15}\ \frac{4}{20}\ \frac{5}{25}\ \frac{6}{30}$

Pages 30-31

A Estimates should be within 1cm
of the answers to section B.

B

1. 5cm   4. 7cm
2. 8cm   5. 10cm
3. 12cm   6. 3cm

Answers

C
1. 10cm	5. 14cm
2. 4cm	6. 3.5cm
3. 2.5cm	7. 6.5cm
4. 11cm	8. 8.5cm

Pages 32-33

A
1. 24	4. 45
2. 21	5. 30
3. 27	6. 56

B
1. 35, 42	5. 9, 18
2. 40, 48	6. 14, 28
3. 60, 54	7. 16, 32
4. 80, 72	8. 18, 36

C
1. 24	4. 2
2. 27	5. 5
3. 3	6. 3, she will have some left over.

D

$2 \times 9 \rightarrow 18$ $4 \times 7 \rightarrow 28$

$6 \times 9 \rightarrow 54$ $9 \times 3 \rightarrow 27$

$\downarrow$ $\downarrow$ $\downarrow$ $\downarrow$

12 81   36 21

Pages 34-35

Answers may be given as digital (12.10) or in the 'o'clock' format.

A
1. 2.10	5. 7.30
2. 4.50	6. 10.15
3. 1.20	7. 3.45
4. 6.05	8. 8.35

B

1. 6.45
2. 8 o'clock
3. 20 minutes

4. 4.25
5. 45 minutes

C
1. 9.05	4. 9.50
2. 9.15	5. 9.55
3. 9.30	6. 10.10

Pages 36-37

A

1. 9 square centimetres
2. 5 square centimetres
3. 7 square centimetres
4. 6 square centimetres
5. 10 square centimetres
6. 6 square centimetres

B

1. 8 square metres
2. 49 square metres
3. 16 square metres
4. 23 square metres
5. 25 square metres

C Check designs are all different and made from 8 squares.

Pages 38-39

A

1. 200 + 70 + 15 = 285
2. 100 + 70 + 18 = 188
3. 200 + 70 + 11 = 281

B
1. 180	2. 244
3. 296	4. 161

C
1. 93	4. 171
2. 83	5. 294
3. 72	6. 251

D
1. 90km	4. 185
2. 67	5. 160
3. 61	6. 174cm

Pages 40-41

A
1. 35	2. 27
3. 26	4. 58

B
1. 5 + 10 = 15	2. 1 + 12 = 13
3. 3 + 14 = 17	4. 4 + 5 = 9

C
1. 20	4. 51
2. 27	5. 15
3. 18	6. 29

D

a) 2	7	b) 1	c) 3	9
2	d) 3	5	6	e) 4
f) 4	1	g) 3	h) 1	5
6	i) 4	7	8	j) 8

Pages 42-43

A

Symmetrical → leaf, TV, ladder
Not symmetrical → car, cup, sock

B

Check each shape drawn is an exact reflection.

C
1. M	4. U
2. B	5. 3
3. X	

Challenge: DECK, CODE, HOOD, WHAT, TOW, HIM

Pages 44-45

Challenge: Three 3-litre jugs and two 4-litre jugs.

A
1. 80 ml	4. 50ml
2. 600ml	5. 200ml
3. 3 litres	6. 1.5 litres

1. 4   2. 2   3. 1   4. 2   5. 1

1. 2	4. 20
2. 10	5. 4
3. 4	6. 5

Pages 46-47

A

1. 56	2. 225
3. 222	4. 174

B

1. 152	2. 184
3. 156	4. 185

C

1. 172	4. 184
2. 141	5. 204
3. 171	6. 140

D

1. 192	4. 144
2. 95km	5. 168 hours
3. 210	6. 177

Pages 48-49

A

1. 16m	4. 24m
2. 28m	5. 18m
3. 22m	6. 32m

B.

1. l 3cm, h 1.5cm, p 9cm
2. l 4cm, h 1cm, p 10cm
3. l 1.5cm, h 1.5cm, p 6cm
4. l 2.5cm, h 3cm, p 11cm
5. l 4cm, h 1.5cm, p 11cm
6. l 2.5cm, h 1cm, p 7cm

C

Rectangle	length	add	height	Multiply total by 2	Perimeter
1	6m	+	2m	= 8 m → x 2	16m
2	8m	+	4m	= 12 m → x 2	24m
3	5m	+	5m	= 10 m → x 2	20m
4	7m	+	9m	= 16 m → x 2	32m
5	11m	+	1m	= 12 m → x 2	24m

Pages 50-51

A Check instructions have been
  followed.
B Check estimated angles are close
  to these:
  1. 150° 2. 110° 3. 90° 4. 45°
  5. 30° 6. 130° 7. 70° 8. 90°
C Check all right angles are
  marked correctly.
D The order should be:
  6 (30°), 4 (45°), 2 (60°),
  1 (100°), 3 (120°), 5 (160°)
Challenge: 32

Pages 52-53

A

1. 9 r 3	4. 8 r 2
2. 6 r 1	5. 5 r 5
3. 7 r 2	6. 6 r 4

B

1. 28	6. 3
2. 9	7. 6
3. 6	8. 8
4. 8	9. 7
5. 3	10. 32

C

1. 11 teams
2. 3 children
3.

17 teams	1 left over
8 teams	3 left over
7 teams	0 left over
5 teams	5 left over
5 teams	0 left over

Challenge: 61

Pages 54-55

A

1. 5	4. 3
2. 3	5. 7
3. 9	

B 12 red, 4 yellow, 8 blue, 6
  large, 3 long

C

1. 7, 14	5. 7, 49
2. 10, 30	6. 4, 28
3. 3, 15	7. 11, 22
4. 2, 16	8. 5, 25

Challenge: 16

Pages 56-57

A

1. 1 kg	4. 3 kg
2. 1 kg	5. $\frac{1}{2}$ kg
3. $\frac{1}{4}$ kg	6. 1 $\frac{1}{2}$ kg

B

1. 2kg	4. 6000g
2. 5000g	5. 9000g
3. 4kg	6. 3kg

C

1. 4kg	4. 7kg
2. 5 $\frac{1}{2}$ kg	5. 8 $\frac{1}{2}$ kg
3. 9 kg	6. 2 $\frac{1}{2}$ kg

Challenge: 4kg

Pages 58-59

A

1. human 2. blue whale
3. hummingbird 4. 35 years
5. cat 6. 10 years
7. leatherback turtle
8. elephant, human and blue
whale

B

1. 10 2. apple 3. orange 4. 7
5. 17 6. 2 7. peach and
pineapple 8. apple and banana
9. 6

Challenge: Bananas are my
  favourite fruit.

Index